# DATE DUE

| | |
|---|---|
| | |
| | |
| | |
| | |
| | |
| | |
| | |
| | |
| | |
| | |
| | |
| | |
| | |
| | |
| | |
| | |
| | |
| | |

The Library Store #47-0119

D1442817

FACT? FICTION?

# Francis Marion

**Cliff Mills**

Mitchell Lane
PUBLISHERS
P.O. Box 196
Hockessin, DE 19707
www.mitchelllane.com

**Mitchell Lane**
PUBLISHERS

Printing     1      2      3      4      5      6      7      8

| | |
|---|---|
| Audie Murphy | **Francis Marion** |
| Buffalo Bill Cody | Robin Hood |
| The Buffalo Soldiers | The Tuskegee Airmen |
| Eliot Ness | Wyatt Earp |

**Library of Congress Cataloging-in-Publication Data**
Mills, Cliff, 1947-
 Francis Marion / by Cliff Mills.
      pages cm. — (Fact or fiction?)
 Includes bibliographical references and index.
 Audience: Grades 3-6.
 ISBN 978-1-61228-948-9 (library bound)
1.  Marion, Francis, 1732–1795—Juvenile literature. 2.  Generals—United States—Biography—Juvenile literature. 3.  South Carolina—Militia—Biography—Juvenile literature. 4.  United States—History—Revolution, 1775–1783--Biography—Juvenile literature. 5.  South Carolina—History—Revolution, 1775–1783—Juvenile literature.  I. Title.
 E207.M3M55 2015
 355.0092—dc23
 [B]

                                              2015003182

eBook ISBN: 978-1-61228-949-6

# CONTENTS

Chapter 1
**A Famous Meeting at Snow's Island**......5

Chapter 2
**Two Heroes in One-The American Robin Hood and the Paul Revere of the South**.................9

Chapter 3
**Guerrilla Warrior**................................15

Chapter 4
**The Fox Leaps Out of the Swamp**..........19

Chapter 5
**A Real Patriot**..............................23

Fact or Fiction? .............................26
Chapter Notes ...............................28
Glossary ...................................30
Works Consulted...........................30
Further Reading ...........................31
On the Internet ............................31
Index .....................................32

Words in **bold** throughout can be found in the Glossary.

A famous painting by John Blake White shows Francis Marion, in the green coat, offering food to a redcoated British officer at a meeting deep in the forest of Snow's Island.

# CHAPTER 1

# A Famous Meeting at Snow's Island

Early one winter morning in 1781, a British Army officer in a bright red coat made his way along the banks of South Carolina's Pee Dee River. He had to watch out for snakes, alligators, and even wolves. After wading through marshes and swamps, he finally reached some higher ground called Snow's Island. Tall pines and cypress trees stood like guards over it. Laurel bushes and vines blocked his way.

Like many British soldiers, he was trying to find the American **patriot** leader Francis Marion. They wanted to kill or capture this fighter for American **independence.**

Marion had spies in the area. He knew the officer was carrying a flag of truce. The Redcoat (as British soldiers were called) was allowed into Marion's well-hidden camp. Marion was dressed in a dark green coat that made him blend into the forest, unlike his visitor.

Marion's men had no uniforms, only old and torn clothes, and a few were barefoot. Some of their swords were made out of old saws. Many of their bullets had been melted down from pewter dinner plates.

The British officer told Marion he wanted to trade prisoners. He would give up patriot prisoners for some

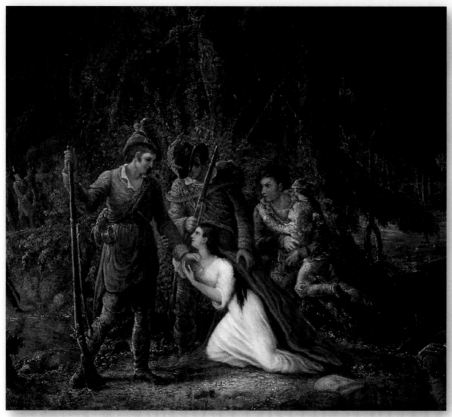

*Another famous painting by John Blake White shows two of Marion's men, holding their rifles, after rescuing a patriot family from British soldiers.*

of the British and **Loyalist** (Americans loyal to the British and King George III) soldiers Marion's men were holding. They made a deal.

Marion's personal servant, a slave named Oscar, was roasting sweet potatoes on a fire. He placed them on a small table made of tree bark. Marion invited the officer to share the meal.

When the Redcoat returned to the British fort in Georgetown, he told his **commander**, "I have seen an American general and his officers, without pay, living on roots and drinking water, and all for LIBERTY!"[1] He didn't believe the British could defeat these men. He resigned from the British Army and joined up with Marion and his men.

This is a famous story of the American Revolutionary War (1775–1783). Artist John Blake White painted the scene in the 1820s. His artwork hangs today in the Senate wing of the US Capitol Building. But the story may be as much fiction as fact.

It first appears in 1804 in a **biography** of Marion by Reverend Mason Locke Weems. Parson Weems, as he is also known, thought his job as a writer was to make heroes. Facts were less important to him than good stories. His first book was about General George Washington. Weems almost certainly made up the story of young George chopping down his father's favorite cherry tree. When that book became a bestseller, Weems chose Marion as his next subject.

Marion's second biographer, William Dobein James, stuck closer to the facts. He makes no mention of the story.[2] And there is no other evidence that any of Marion's men was an ex-British officer. However, there is good evidence that a British officer visited Marion in the woods, at some location.[3] As is often the case, fact and fiction mingle and it is hard to separate them. And a good story has a way of living on, especially when someone paints it and hangs it in the US Senate.

Snow Island, deep in an area of cypress swamps and wetlands, was Francis Marion's favorite hiding place.

# CHAPTER 2

# Two Heroes in One–
## The American Robin Hood and
## the Paul Revere of the South

We know some facts about Francis Marion. He was born in 1732 (or close to that year) in what is now Berkeley County, South Carolina. When he was five or six years old, his family moved to a large farm, a plantation, near Georgetown, South Carolina.

As a young man, he fought against Indians (mostly Cherokee) who were threatening the western portion of the Carolinas during the French and Indian War (1754–1763), gaining invaluable experience. "The Cherokee used the landscape to their advantage, Marion found; they concealed themselves in the Carolina backwoods and mounted devastating ambushes," according to *Smithsonian* magazine. "Two decades later, Marion would apply these tactics against the British."[1]

When the Revolutionary War began, he became a captain in the 2nd South Carolina Regiment, a state **militia**—volunteer armies raised by each colony. He was a good and disciplined soldier, so was quickly promoted to major and then lieutenant colonel. He commanded Fort Sullivan in Charleston, South Carolina, and helped keep the city out of the hands of the British for several years.

The facts now begin to compete with fiction. One of the sources of fiction about Marion is a Disney series called *The Swamp Fox* that ran for eight episodes from 1959 to 1961 and starred Leslie Nielsen. Nielsen's Marion was tall, handsome, witty, and charming, wooing girlfriend Mary Videau. The real Marion was short, not handsome, and was not known for being witty or charming.

Introducing the series, Walt Disney tells the television audience it is spring 1780 and the American Revolution is in danger of failing. But there is a hero: Francis Marion is "the American Robin Hood" who will save the revolution. In the first scene, Marion is fast and furious as he rides to warn the people of Charleston that the British are coming. He is a southern Paul Revere. Marion arrives at an American officer's party with the news. The drunken partiers don't believe him. The host officer, probably a Loyalist who is trying to distract the Americans from the approaching danger, attacks him with a sword. Marion runs upstairs and jumps out a window to escape. He hurts his ankle.

The historical facts line up much differently. Some 150 British warships had been in Charleston harbor for several weeks.[2] The harbor looked like a forest of masts. The real Marion attended a party in Charleston on March 19, 1780, at an American officer's house. Marion did not like parties and drinking. The only way he could escape was to jump out the second floor, but he broke his ankle. There was no officer trying to fight him. And everyone had known the British were coming. They were already there.

*The port of Charleston, South Carolina was the scene of many battles, including this British attack on Fort Sullivan in 1776. The flag of South Carolina in the upper left still flies, in a battle the patriots won.*

What happened next is clear. On May 9, the British ships started an all-out bombardment of Charleston. The city and its forts surrendered three days later. Thousands of American **Continental Army** (the national army) and state militia soldiers were captured, along with seven generals. Ten warships, hundreds of cannons, and thousands of muskets were also taken by the British. It was to be the worst day in American military history until World War II.[3]

For the patriots, the fall of Charleston was terrible news. They were fighting to have a better government and a better life. The Loyalists thought it was great news. Many were afraid they would lose their lands if the British left.

Marion was not captured in Charleston because he was still recovering away from the city. After the news spread throughout South Carolina, small groups of "irregular" patriot fighters begin to form. They were not part of the Continental Army or the state militia. One group formed near Georgetown. They were farmers, blacksmiths, coopers (barrel makers), leatherworkers, and more. They found a leader in Marion. He wasn't a Robin Hood, urging them to steal from the rich and give to the poor. He didn't want to help one king and hurt another as Robin Hood did. He wanted America to be free from all kings.

Another irregular patriot group formed in western South Carolina. Thomas Sumter was its leader. His house had been burned to the ground by the British and Loyalists while his wife watched from her wheelchair. Sumter's men gathered in a secret camp off the Catawba River and trained in hand-to-hand fighting, the mixed martial arts of the day.

A civil war in the South began. Loyalist and patriot bands became "night riders," attacking each other. Marion and his men joined in the fight for people's hearts and minds.

General George Washington had sent a part of the Continental Army to the South, knowing the British were going to focus the war there. It was led by General Horatio Gates and included both experienced and inexperienced fighters. Marion and his men rode into their camp in early August 1780. A Continental

Army officer described them: "Col. Marion, a gentleman of South Carolina [had] a very few followers…their number did not exceed twenty men and boys, some white, some black and all mounted [on horseback], but most of them miserably equipped."[4] The army officers had to stop the soldiers from laughing at Marion and his men. Gates sent Marion and his men away to spy on the British and destroy boats near by.

Soon after, on August 16, British forces led by General Charles Cornwallis used the shock and awe of cannons, **sabers** (swords), and bayonets to tear through Gates's army in the Battle of Camden. The inexperienced militia forces were no match for Cornwallis. The clash of steel on steel often meant that another American was killed or wounded that day.

Marion and his men were about ten miles away from the battle, and possibly could hear the cannons and see the smoke. Once again, Marion had been within miles of a terrible patriot defeat. He was now forced to became a different kind of fighter—a **guerrilla**. Guerrilla warfare means striking the enemy and disappearing before they can catch you. It is also known as **partisan** warfare.

The Marion legend was about to begin. Much of it is based on what Marion did in the months following the Battle of Camden.

*For most of his adult life, Marion led the quiet life of a gentleman farmer and a politician who helped write the South Carolina constitution.*

# Guerrilla Warrior

Amajor monument is being planned to honor Marion in Washington, DC. The website description states that Marion "is generally credited as the Father of Guerilla Warfare."[1] This belief is an important part of the Marion legend.

Yet this kind of fighting had been around a very long time. Calling Marion "the father of guerrilla warfare" is more fiction than fact. Even in Marion's time he was called "the Fabius of South Carolina."[2] Fabius was a Roman general who followed the invader Hannibal for years in Italy in the 200s BCE (Before the Common Era). Fabius knew that an army away from home and supply lines for a long time would be weakened. So he didn't confront Hannibal directly in major battles, but rather chipped away at his enemy in a series of smaller attacks. Jewish rebels used similar tactics against the Romans in Judea in the first century CE (Common Era). In America, Major Robert Rogers employed guerrilla tactics in the French and Indian War.

In fact, Marion may not even have been the first South Carolinian credited with being a guerrilla warrior. John W. Gordon, a professor of national security affairs

*At the Battle of Camden, British cavalrymen armed with sabers and foot soldiers with bayonets were deadly, killing Continental Army troops and forcing some militia to run for their lives.*

at the US Marine Corps Command in Quantico, Virginia, notes that "Thomas Sumter . . . had been the first to take the field in this new partisan phase [after the Battle of Camden]."[3]

The Marion Memorial website also states that, after the Battle of Camden, Marion and his band of irregulars were "the only organized fighting force in action in America."[4] But Gordon notes that, after

Camden, "The Americans had no body of organized troops left in South Carolina."[5] So calling Marion's men an "organized fighting force" might be a stretch.

Marion's first guerrilla **skirmish** took place on August 20, four days after the Battle of Camden. The British were bringing some of their prisoners to Charleston. Marion found out that some were being held near Nelson's Ferry, on the Santee River. The British officers were celebrating in a tavern called the Blue House. The Redcoats' guns were stacked in a nearby field. Marion divided his men into two groups. He handed out white cockades, badges made of ribbons. This way they would tell friend from foe, since some were new to the fighting.

*Thomas Sumter is another Revolutionary War hero, known as the "Fighting Carolina Gamecock" for his guerrilla attacks on British soldiers in South Carolina.*

Marion's men attacked after dark. Some terrified officers hid in the tavern, and many Loyalists with the British ran into the forest to escape. Marion set free about 150 American prisoners. His men also captured muskets, bayonets, and ammunition.

Marion and his men were a small mobile fighting force, often using flat-bottomed boats to get across the Pee Dee and other rivers.

# CHAPTER 4

# The Fox Leaps Out of the Swamp

Many people are familiar with the "Swamp Fox" story. Marion and his men rise out of the swamps, strike the British and Loyalists, and disappear back into the swamps. The Disney series, the Marion Memorial, and much of our memory of Marion are based on this idea.

But it is only partly factual. Marion was never called "The Swamp Fox" in his day. The term originated with Weems's book. One day, writes Weems, two young ladies and some British officers were out riding near Georgetown in a "courting party,"[1] a sort of group date. As they got further away from town and into the woods, the girls began shaking. They said they were worried "that vile [evil] 'swamp fox,' as they called Marion . . . [could] come across them."[2] As usual with Weems, we can't be sure the story is true. But the term "Swamp Fox" didn't catch on until Marion's third biographer, William Gilmore Simms, used it in the 1840s.[3] By then Marion had been dead for nearly 50 years.

Marion may well have hated swamps. He wrote in a letter to Gates that when he chased a group of Loyalists into the swamps at Blue Savannah, the swamps "were **impassible** [blocked] to all but Tories [another name for Loyalists]."[4]

The facts show that, for many skirmishes, Marion's men drove enemy forces *into* the swamps rather than attacking *from* the swamps. For example, on September 4, Marion and a few men ambushed Loyalists near the Pee Dee River at Blue Savannah. The Loyalists ran into the swamps to escape. The same thing happened late the following month. Marion's spies told him that a Loyalist force was camped next to a road running near Tearcoat Swamp. His scouts watched the Loyalists playing cards and listening to music. There were no guards or sentries.[5] Just before midnight, Marion and his men struck. The Loyalists panicked and some ran into Tearcoat Swamp. Marion didn't follow them.

By now, Marion had become a real problem for Cornwallis, making the road from Camden to Charleston dangerous. So Cornwallis sent his best officer, Lt. Colonel Banastre Tarleton, looking for Marion on a "search and destroy" mission.

Tarleton led the **British Legion**, one of the top British fighting units, composed of the best Loyalist **cavalry** and **infantry**. Their heavy sabers (swords) could cut off an arm with a single swing.

For weeks in late 1780, Marion and Tarleton laid traps for each other. Each was too smart to get ambushed. Then one day, Tarleton chased Marion and his men along Jack's Creek and the Black River for seven hours, over 25 miles or more. Finally, Tarleton reached Ox Swamp and gave up. He famously turned to his men and said, "Let us go back, and we will soon find the game cock [his nickname for Sumter], but as for this damned old fox [Marion], the devil himself could not catch him."[6]

Tarleton did not use the word "swamp." In fact, Marion was not hiding in a swamp. He was at a place called Benboo's Ferry. He and his men had made a log defense and were waiting for a battle with Tarleton that never came. If it had, there is a good chance Francis Marion would have died that day.

Facts also show that some of the most important battles Marion won had nothing to do with swamps and guerrilla warfare, but with capturing key British forts by **siege**. American General Nathanael Greene teamed Marion up with Colonel Henry Lee (father of the famous Confederate General Robert E. Lee) in early 1781. They and their mix of regular and irregular soldiers captured two British forts, Watson and Motte. Their men built a tower for sharpshooters at one siege and dug miles of trenches at the other.

Marion's legend is short-changed when it limits him to the swamps. He could fight on any ground. He was also an accomplished intelligence officer for General Greene, reporting on Loyalist troop movements and losses in combat.[7] Marion was also a good forager for supplies for Greene's army in the summer of 1781. He brought corn, rice, salt, and cattle to the hungry soldiers.[8] He was therefore much more than just a swamp fox.

*Daniel Morgan may have been the real inspiration for the hero in the movie* The Patriot, *since he used fighting tactics similar to those used by patriot Benjamin Martin in the movie.*

# A Real Patriot

Some of our most recent ideas about Marion come from the movie *The Patriot* (2000). Screenwriter Robert Rodat told reporter Rick Lyman of *The New York Times* that the script was originally based on Marion. But he also used a combination of other Revolutionary War figures.[1] Nevertheless, most reviewers and moviegoers seem to think it is largely based on Marion.[2]

In the movie, South Carolina patriot Benjamin Martin (played by Mel Gibson) doesn't want to go to war against the British. He needs to protect his large family. His children's mother has died. But after the evil British Colonel Tavington (Jason Isaacs) kills one of his sons, Martin is drawn into a frenzy of bloody fighting. He commands a small army near the end of the movie, and wins one of the biggest battles of the war. That battle is based on the famous American victory at Cowpens, South Carolina, in early 1781.

However, not much of the movie seems based on Marion. He did not have any children. He was not reluctant to get into the war. There is no evidence that he was a specialist in hand-to-hand combat, drenching himself in enemy blood as he swung his tomahawk. The real Marion was small and slight, and favored an old **cutlass** (a short sword). He never commanded an army in a traditional battle.

So who was the movie based on? As Rodat said, many people. Patriot leader Andrew Pickens had a large family and didn't want to get into the war. Both Thomas Sumter and Daniel Morgan would have known bloody hand-to-hand fighting. Morgan was the true hero of the Battle of Cowpens. A cousin of the legendary Daniel Boone, he was a powerfully built man with a deep scar on his face from an Indian bullet. Just before the battle at Cowpens, he told the militiamen, "Just hold your heads up, boys, three fires [take three shots] and you are free."[3] He told them the girls would kiss them when they got home. His tactics helped win the day in one of the most important battles in American history.

One scene in the movie shows Colonel Tavington locking many women, children, and older men in a church and setting fire to it, killing them all. Tavington is clearly based on Tarleton, but there is no evidence that Tarleton did something similar. But Tarleton could be cruel and bloodthirsty. At one battle, the average American patriot had sixteen wounds from Tarleton and his men.[4]

But the movie does capture something important about Marion. He never gave up. He overcame setback after setback. Many history books quote a letter from American General Nathanael Greene to a French minister: "We fight, get beat, rise, and fight again."[5] Marion fought, rose, and fought again. He won by not losing.

And, like Benjamin Martin, he was ruthless and effective when he needed to be. He got things done. He was a good military strategist. He was effective not only as a guerrilla fighter, but also as a soldier in the Continental Army and the state militia. Lord Cornwallis complained that Marion used "terror and punishment" to make patriots out of Loyalists.[6] But that was a sign that Marion was winning the battle for hearts and minds that Cornwallis and the British were losing.

Marion was tough, but he was also a forgiving man. More than once he stopped his own men from hanging a Loyalist. After the war, he fought for the rights of Loyalists when he was in the South Carolina legislature. He believed they had suffered enough in this first American civil war.

The Marion Memorial website is right about several things. Francis Marion is a national hero whose name is found on many cities and counties throughout America.[7] He was more than a swamp fox. He was a good soldier, equal parts tough and merciful.

The cause of independence didn't depend on one or two people. It depended on many. We should honor as many as we can, including Oscar, his slave, and others like him. We should honor the women who saw the power of the idea for American independence before the men in their lives did. And we should honor Marion, who never wanted glory, just freedom.

# FACT OR FICTION?

FICTION: Marion was a southern Paul Revere.

FACT: Marion didn't need to warn the citizens of Charleston that the British were coming. The citizens could look out into the harbor.

WHY IT MATTERS: Much of the history of the American Revolutionary War has been written by scholars in the North even though a vital part of the war was fought in the South. Marion doesn't need to be compared to a legend from Boston.

FICTION: Marion was the father of guerrilla warfare.

FACT: Marion wasn't the first to use guerrilla tactics, and may not have even been the first in South Carolina. Some experts believe Thomas Sumter preceded him.

WHY IT MATTERS: Guerrilla warfare is an important part of world affairs today, and understanding its roots and methods is important.

FICTION: Marion was called the "Swamp Fox" during his lifetime.

FACT: William Gilmore Simms created the "Swamp Fox" nickname in the 1840s.

WHY IT MATTERS: Marion's legend should be about much more than his swamp fox days. He was a good soldier who served his country in many ways.

FICTION: The movie *The Patriot* was based on Marion's life.

FACT: Very little of Benjamin Martin's life is similar to Marion's.

WHY IT MATTERS: Marion used surprise and smart military tactics to achieve his goals, not brute force.

FICTION: A British soldier brought a truce flag, saw Marion's men, and resigned to join them because he was so moved by their cause.

FACT: A British officer did visit Marion, but there is no evidence that he joined Marion.

WHY IT MATTERS: The Revolutionary War wasn't won by British soldiers joining American patriots.

## Chapter 1: A Famous Meeting at Snow's Island

1. Steven D. Smith, "Imagining the Swamp Fox: William Gilmore Simms and the National Memory of Francis Marion." *William Gilmore Simms Unfinished Civil War: Consequences for a Southern Man of Letters*, ed. David Moltke-Hansen (Columbia, SC: University of South Carolina Press, 2013), p. 40.
2. Ibid.
3. United States Senate, "General Marion Inviting a British Officer to Share His Meal." http://www.senate.gov.artsandhistory/art/artifact/Painting_33_htm

## Chapter 2: Two Heroes in One—The American Robin Hood and the Paul Revere of the South

1. Amy Crawford, "The Swamp Fox: Elusive and Crafty, Francis Marion Outwitted British Troops During the American Revolution." *Smithsonian Magazine*, June 30, 2007. http://www.smithsonianmag.com/biography/the-swamp-fox-157330429.html
2. Charles Bracelen *Flood, Rise, and Fight Again: Perilous Times Along the Road to Independence* (New York: Dodd, Mead, and Company, 1976), p. 257.
3. Ibid.
4. Ibid., p. 285.

## Chapter 3: Guerrilla Warrior

1. Francis Marion Memorial, "The Legend of the Swamp Fox." http://www.swampfoxmemorial.org
2. Steven D. Smith, "Imagining the Swamp Fox: William Gilmore Simms and the National Memory of Francis Marion." *William Gilmore Simms Unfinished Civil War: Consequences for a Southern Man of Letters*, ed. David Moltke-Hansen (Columbia, SC: University of South Carolina Press, 2013), p. 44.
3. John Gordon, *South Carolina and the American Revolution* (Columbia, SC: University of South Carolina Press, 2003), p. 44.
4. Francis Marion Memorial.
5. Gordon, p. 95.

## Chapter 4: The Fox Leaps Out of the Swamp

1. Steven D. Smith, "Imagining the Swamp Fox: William Gilmore Simms and the National Memory of Francis Marion." William Gilmore Simms *Unfinished Civil War: Consequences for a Southern Man of Letters*, ed. David Moltke-Hansen (Columbia, SC: University of South Carolina Press, 2013), p. 36.
2. Ibid.
3. Ibid, p. 37.
4. Ibid, p. 39.
5. John Gordon, *South Carolina and the American Revolution* (Columbia, SC: University of South Carolina Press, 2003), p. 118.
6. Smith, p. 37.
7. George Kyle, "Francis Marion as an Intelligence Officer." *The South Carolina Historical Magazine*, October 1976. http://www.jstor.org/stable27567404.html
8. Ibid.

## Chapter 5: A Real Patriot

1. Rick Lyman, "At the Movies: It's Not War, It's Principles." *The New York Times*, June 23, 2000. http://www.nytimes.com/2000/06/23/movies/at-the-movies-it-s-not-war-it-s-principles.html
2. Jay Carr, "Mel Gibson Shows His Brave Heart in 'The Patriot.'" *The Boston Globe*, June 28, 2000.
3. Barbara W. Tuchman, *The First Salute* (New York: Ballantine Books, 1988), p. 207.
4. Charles Bracelen Flood, *Rise, and Fight Again: Perilous Times Along the Road to Independence* (New York: Dodd, Mead, and Company, 1976), p. 261.
5. Flood, p. 399.
6. Tuchman, p. 207.
7. Francis Marion Memorial, "The Legend of the Swamp Fox." http://www.swampfoxmemorial.org/francismarion.html

**biography** (buy-AHG-ra-fee)—the story of a person's life, written by another person

**British Legion** (BRIT-ish LEE-jun)—a Loyalist American force formed in 1778 with roughly 250 soldiers on horse and 200 on foot

**cavalry** (KAV-uhl-ree)—soldiers mounted on horseback

**commander** (kom-MAN-duhr)—a person in charge, often an officer of high rank

**Continental Army** (kahn-tin-EHN-tull ARM-ee)—the American national army created on June 14, 1775, by the Continental Congress

**cutlass** (CUT-liss)—a short heavy sword with a curved blade, often used by sailors and pirates

**impassible** (im-PASS-ah-bull)—an area that is hard or impossible to get through

**independence** (in-dee-PEN-dense)—gaining freedom from control by others

**infantry** (IN-fan-tree)—soldiers on foot

**Loyalist** (LOY-uhl-ist)—person who remained loyal to the English crown

**militia** (mi-LISH-uh)—usually unpaid volunteer soldiers

**partisan** (PAHR-tuh-zuhn)—lightly armed troops who harass an enemy

**patriot** (PAY-tree-ott)—person who strongly supports his or her country

**plantation** (plan-TAY-shun)—a large area of land where crops like rice or cotton are grown

**Redcoat** (RED-cote)—British soldier, who usually wore a red coat as part of his uniform

**saber** (SAY-burr)—long heavy sword with a curved blade

**siege** (SEEJ)—soldiers surrounding a fort or building for long periods of time, in order to take control

**skirmish** (SKUR-mish)—a brief and unplanned fight

## WORKS CONSULTED

Axelrod, Alan. *The Real History of the American Revolution*. New York: Sterling Publishing, 2007.

Carr, Jay. "Mel Gibson Shows a Brave Heart in the 'Patriot.'" *The Boston Globe*, June 28, 2000.

Crawford, Amy. "The Swamp Fox: Elusive and Crafty, Francis Marion Outwitted British Troops During the American Revolution." *Smithsonian Magazine*, June 30, 2007. http://www.smithsonianmag.com/biography/the-swamp-fox-157330429.html

Edgar, Walter. *Partisans and Redcoats: The Southern Conflict That Turned the Tide of the American Revolution*. New York: HarperCollins, 2001.

Flood, Charles Bracelen. *Rise, and Fight Again*. NY: Dodd, Mead, and Company, 1976.

Fowler, William M. *American Crisis: George Washington and the Dangerous Two Years After Yorktown*. New York: Walker Publishing, 2011.

Francis Marion Memorial. "The Legend of Swamp Fox."
   http://www.swampfoxmemorial.org/francismarion.html
Gordon, John W. *South Carolina and the American Revolution*. Columbia, SC:
   University of South Carolina Press, 2003.
Harvey, Robert. *A Few Bloody Noses: The Realities and Mythologies of the American Revolution*.Woodstock, New York: Overlook Press, 2001.
Kyle, George. "Francis Marion as an Intelligence Officer." *The South Carolina Historical Magazine*, October 1976. http://www.jstor.org/stable27567404.html
Lyman, Rick. "At the Movies: It's Not War, It's Principles." *The New York Times*, June 23, 2000. http://www.nytimes.com/2000/06/23/
   movies/at-the-movies-it-s-not-war-it-s-principles.html
Scotti, Anthony J. *Brutal Virtue: The Myth and Reality of Banastre Tarleton*. Bowie, MD: Heritage Books, 2002.
Smith, Steven D. "Imagining the Swamp Fox: William Gilmore Simms and the National Memory of Francis Marion." *William Gilmore Simms Unfinished Civil War: Consequences for a Southern Man of Letters*. Ed. David Moltke-Hansen. Columbia, SC: University of South Carolina Press, 2013.
Townsend, Kenneth. *South Carolina*. Northampton, MA: Interlink Books, 2009.
Tuchman, Barbara W. *The First Salute*. New York: Ballantine Books, 1988.
United State Senate. "General Marion Inviting a British Officer to Share His Meal." http://www.senate.gov/artandhistory/art/artifact/Painting_33_htm
Weems, Parson M.L. and Brigadier General P. Horry. *The Life of General Francis Marion*. Winston-Salem, NC: John Blair, 2000.
Wood, Gordon. *The Idea of America*. New York: Penguin Press, 2011.

## FURTHER READING

Bodie, Idella. *The Revolutionary Swamp Fox*. Orangeburg, SC: Sandpaper Publishing, 1999.
Cornelius, Kay. *Francis Marion: The Swamp Fox*. Broomall, PA: Chelsea House Publishers, 2001.
Murray, Aaron, editor. *American Revolution: Battles and Leaders*. New York: DK Publishing, 2004.
Palmer, Kate Sally. *Francis Marion and the Legend of the Swamp Fox*. Central, SC: Warbranch Press, 2005.

## ON THE INTERNET

Francis Marion Trail
   http://www.francismariontrial.com
National Park Service, Marion Park
   http://www.nps.gov/cahi/learn/historyculture/cahi_marion_htm
Pee Dee Explorer
   http://www.scetv.org/index/php/pee_dee_explorer/entry/the_swamp_fox

Benboo's Ferry   21
Berkeley County   9
Black River   20
Blue House   17
Blue Savannah   19, 20
Boone, Daniel   24
British Legion   20
Camden, Battle of   13, 16, 17
cavalry   20
Continental Army   11, 12, 13, 25
Cornwallis, General Charles
     13, 25
Cowpens, Battle of   23
cutlass   24
Fabius   15
Fort Motte   21
Fort Sullivan   9, 11
Fort Watson   21
French and Indian War   9, 15
Gates, Horatio   12, 13
Georgetown   6, 9, 12, 19
Gordon, John   15
Greene, Nathaniel   21, 25
Gibson, Mel   23
guerrilla fighting   13, 15
Hannibal   15
independence   5
infantry   20
Isaacs, Jason   23
Jack's Creek   20
James, Willian Dobein   7

Jewish rebels   15
Lee, Henry   21
Loyalist   6, 10, 12, 17, 19, 20, 25
Marion memorial   19, 25
Martin, Benjamin   23
militia   11, 12
Morgan, Daniel   22, 23, 24
Nielsen, Leslie   10
Nelson's Ferry   17
night riders   12
Oscar   6, 26
Ox Swamp   20
*Patriot, The*   23, 27
Pee Dee River   5, 18
Revolutionary War   7, 9
Rogers, Robert   15
sabers   20
Santee River   17
siege   21
Simms, William Gilmore   19, 27
Snow's Island   5
South Carolina Regiment   9
Sumter, Thomas   12, 16, 26
Swamp Fox   19, 21
*Swamp Fox* (TV series)   10
Tarleton, Banastre   20, 22, 24
Tearcoat Swamp   20
Videau, Mary   10
Washington, George   7, 12
Weems, Mason Locke   7, 19
White, John Blake   4, 6, 7

## ABOUT THE AUTHOR

Cliff Mills is a writer and editor living in Jacksonville, Florida. He has written biographies of many world leaders, such as Hannibal, Angela Merkel, and Pope Benedict XVI. He has also written about sports and entertainment figures. Cliff has been a lifelong student of the American Revolutionary War. He has a special interest because one of his ancestors fought in it at the age of 16.